Disney
MALEFICENT

ISBN 978-1-4803-9834-4

Disney characters and artwork © Disney Enterprises, Inc.

Walt Disney Music Company
Wonderland Music Company, Inc.

DISTRIBUTED BY

HAL•LEONARD®
CORPORATION

7777 W. BLUEMOUND RD. P.O. BOX 13819 MILWAUKEE, WI 53213

In Australia Contact:
Hal Leonard Australia Pty. Ltd.
4 Lentara Court
Cheltenham, Victoria, 3192 Australia
Email: ausadmin@halleonard.com.au

Visit Hal Leonard Online at
www.halleonard.com

WELCOME TO THE MOORS

By JAMES NEWTON HOWARD

Moderately fast, in 2

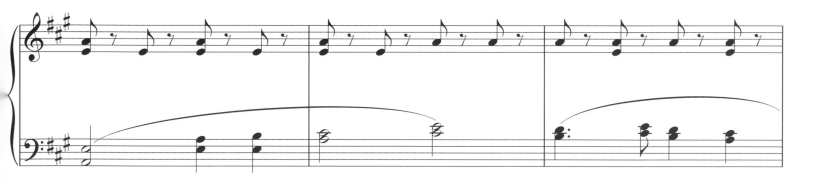

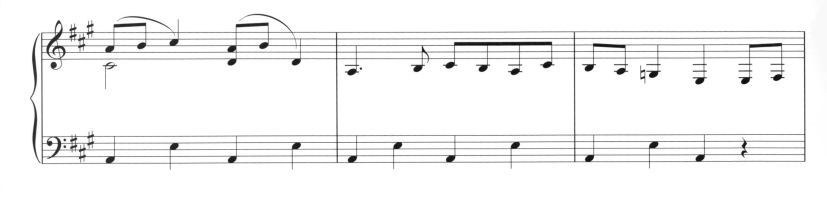

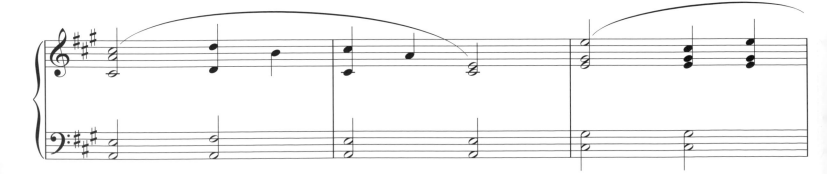

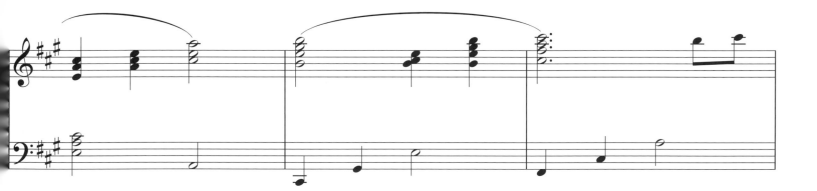

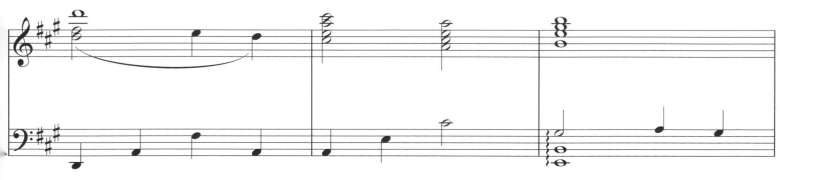

MALEFICENT SUITE

By JAMES NEWTON HOWARD

PRINCE PHILLIP

By JAMES NEWTON HOWARD

Slowly, freely

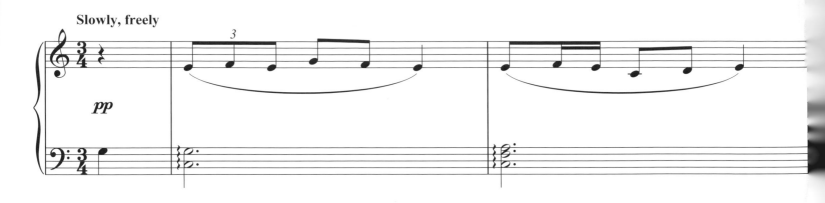

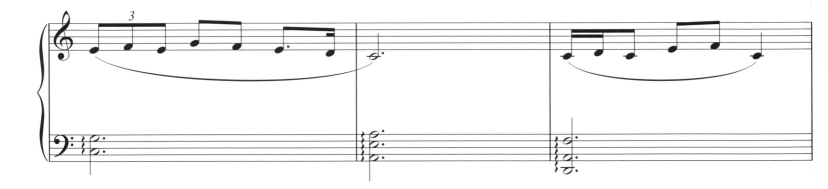

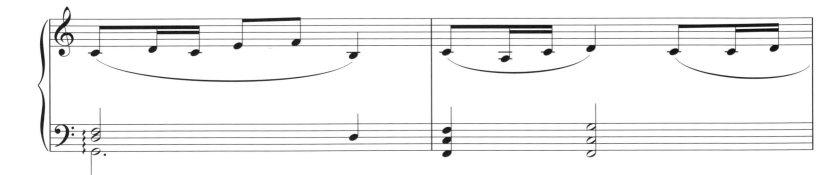

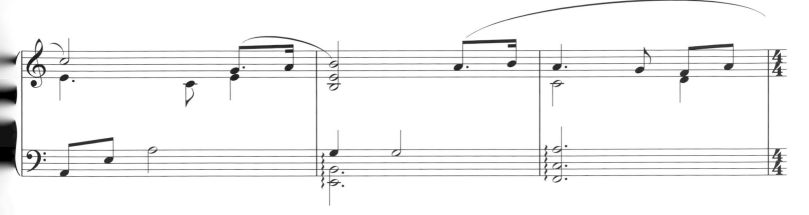

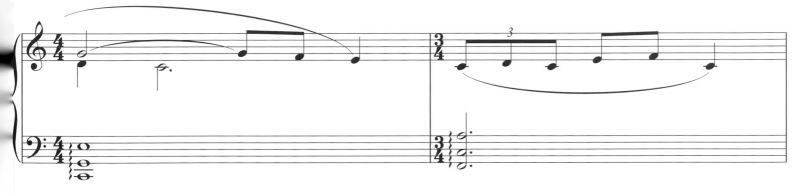

AURORA IN FAERIELAND

By JAMES NEWTON HOWARD

Slowly, expressively

Pedal ad lib. throughout

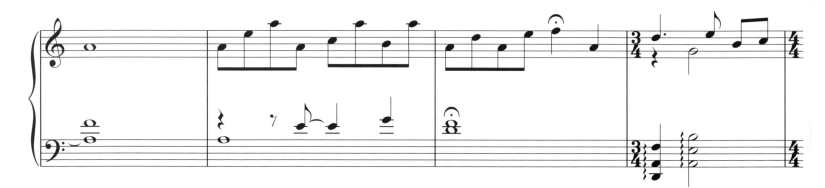

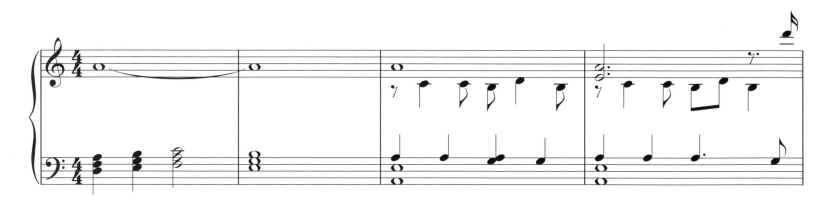

rit.   *a tempo*

PHILLIP'S KISS

By JAMES NEWTON HOWARD

Slowly, expressively

Pedal ad lib. throughout

Moderately fast, steadily

Tempo I

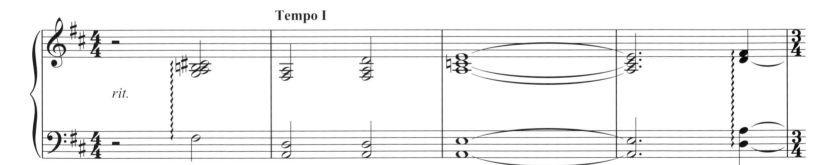

Slightly faster

TRUE LOVE'S KISS

By JAMES NEWTON HOWARD

Moderately slow, expressively

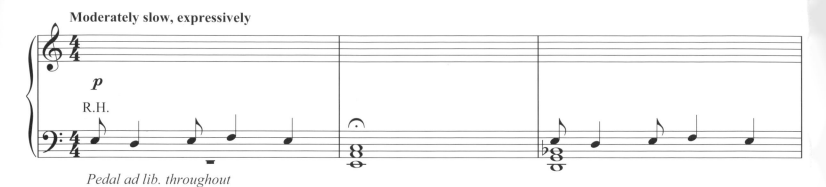

Pedal ad lib. throughout

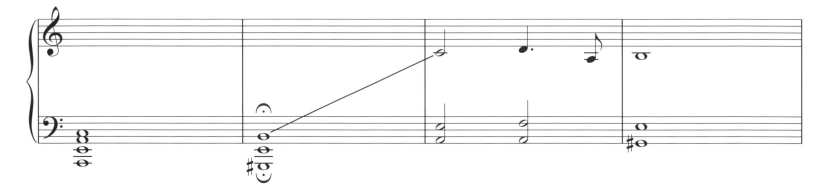

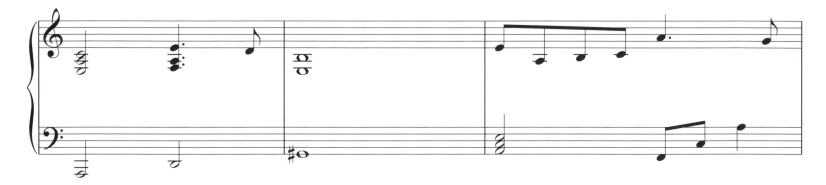

23

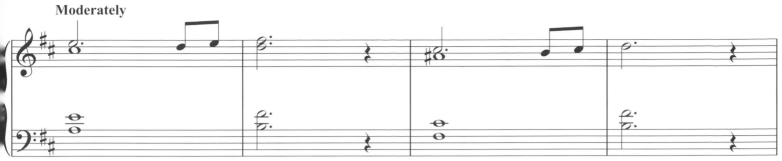

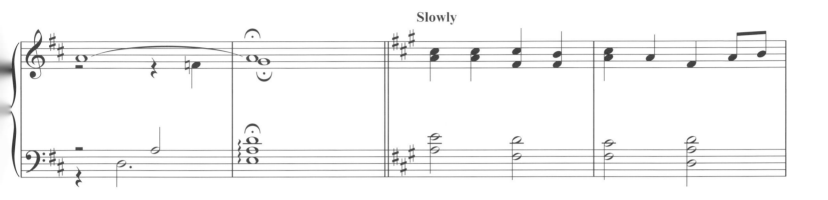

ARE YOU MALEFICENT?

By JAMES NEWTON HOWARD

Moderately, expressively

p

Pedal ad lib. throughout

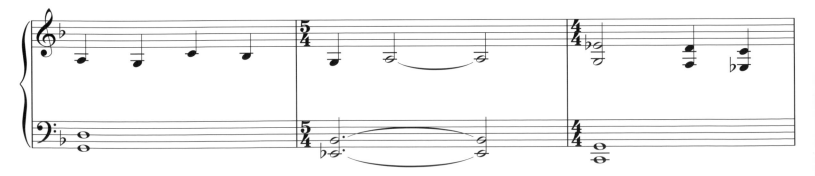

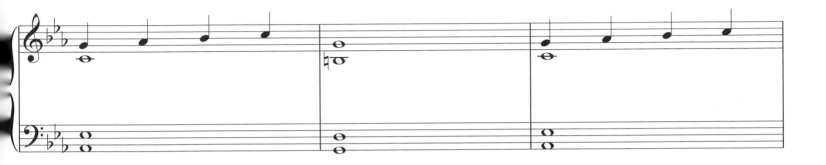

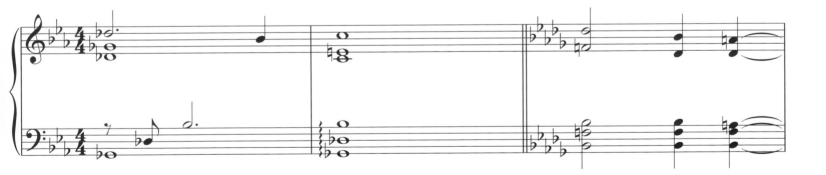

Moderately fast, steadily

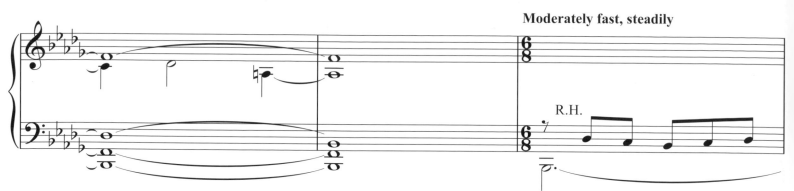

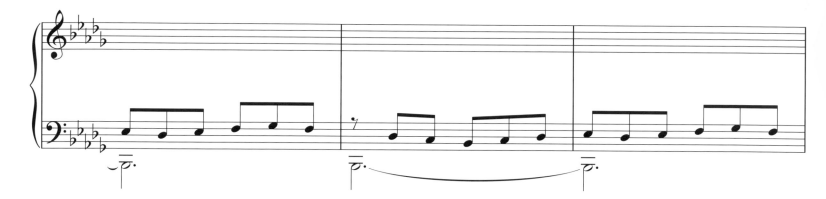

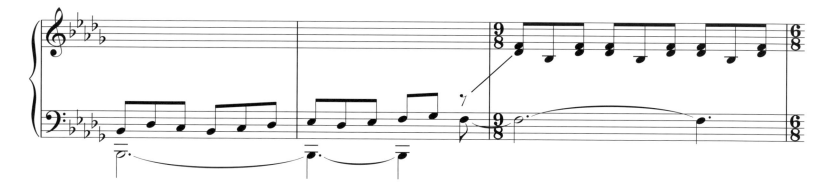

MALEFICENT IS CAPTURED

By James Newton Howard

Moderately

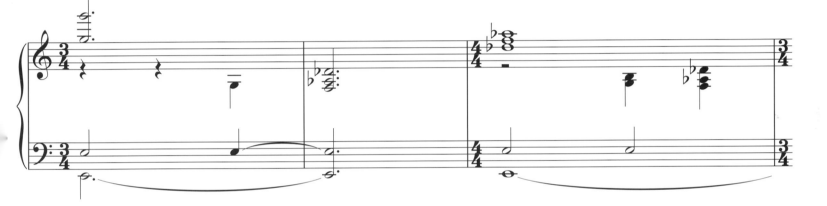

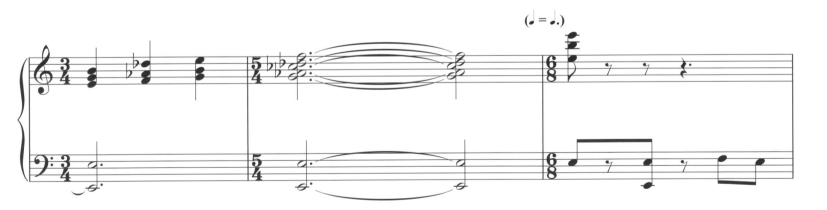

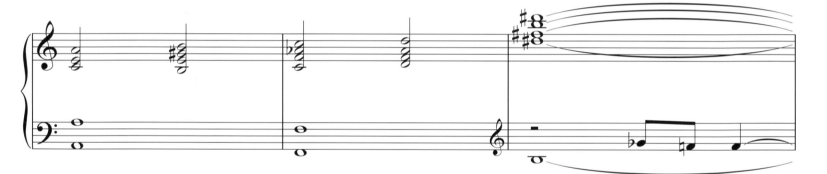

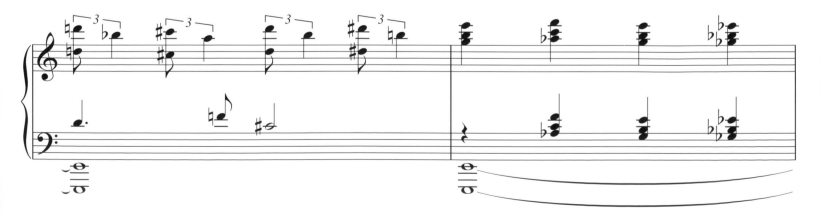

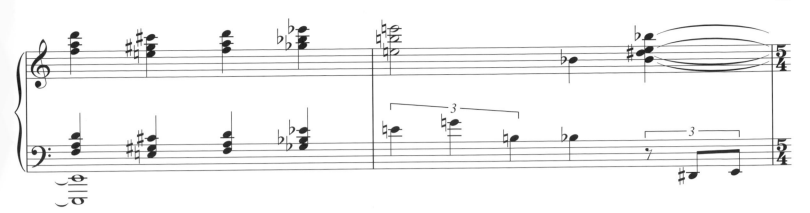

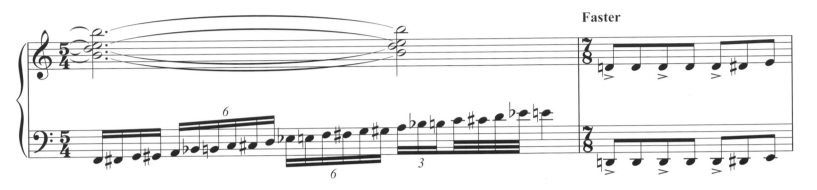

THE QUEEN OF FAERIELAND

By JAMES NEWTON HOWARD

Slowly, expressively

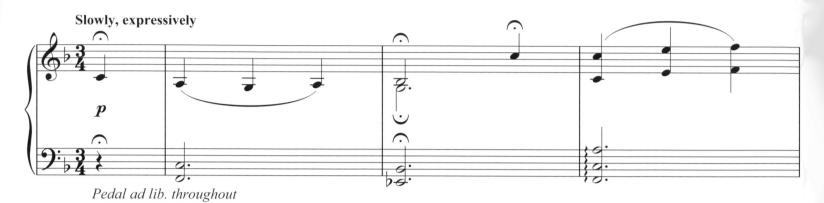

p

Pedal ad lib. throughout

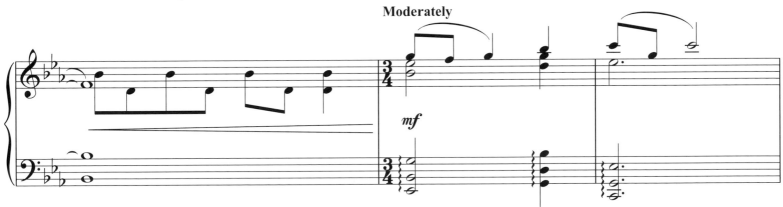

Moderately

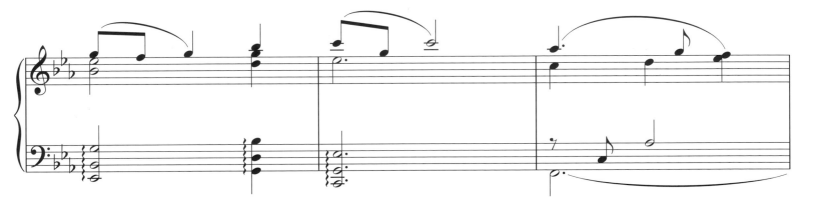

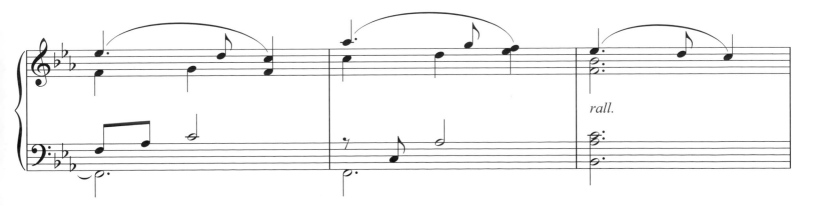

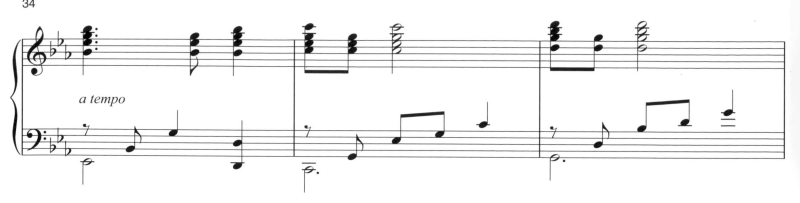

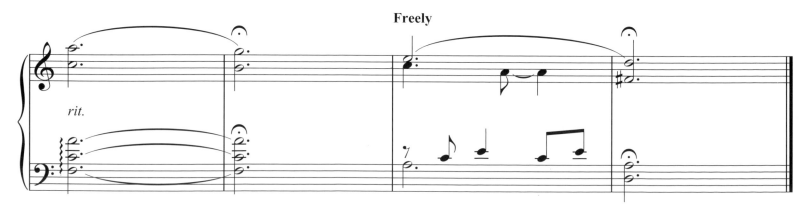

ONCE UPON A DREAM

Words and Music by SAMMY FAIN
and JACK LAWRENCE
Adapted from a Theme by TCHAIKOVSKY

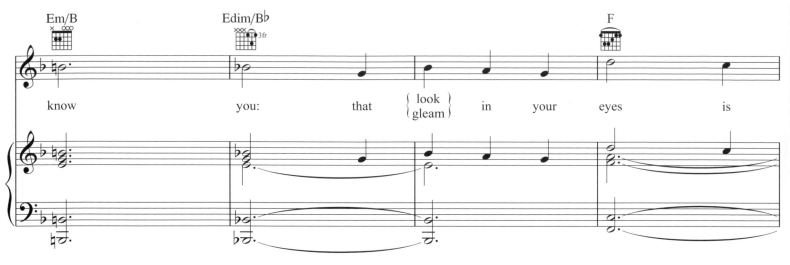

know you: that ${look \atop gleam}$ in your eyes is

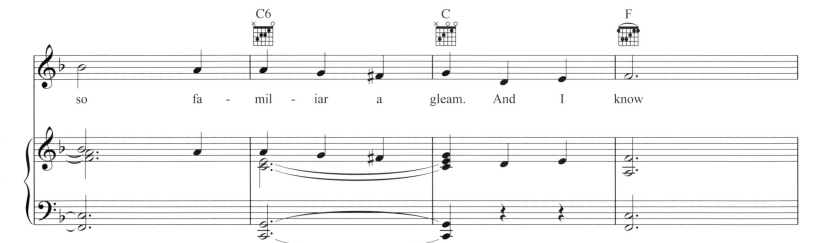

so fa - mil - iar a gleam. And I know

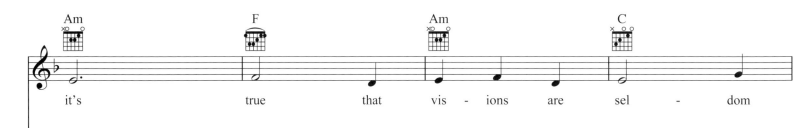

it's true that vis - ions are sel - dom

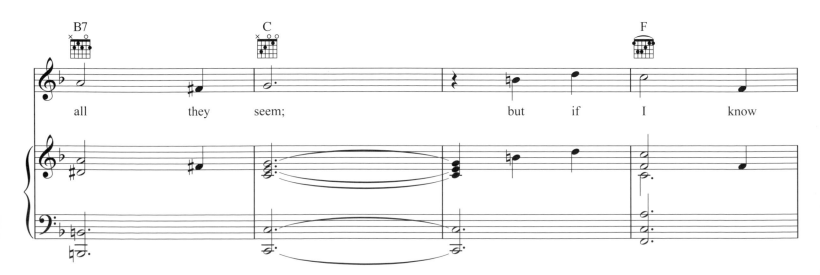

all they seem; but if I know

you,   I   know   what   you'll   do: you'll

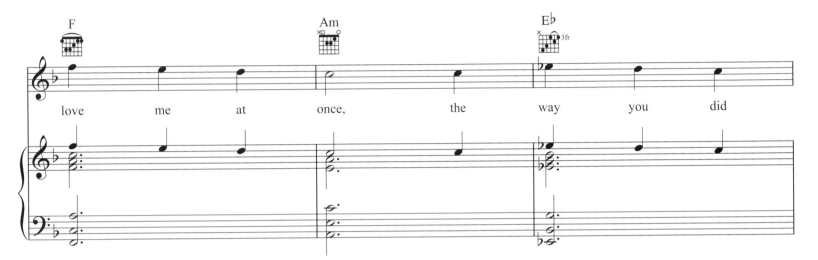

love   me   at   once,   the   way   you   did

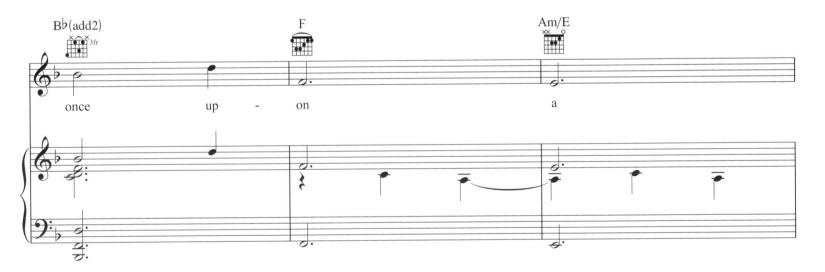

once   up - on   a

dream.   Ah, _____   ah, _____

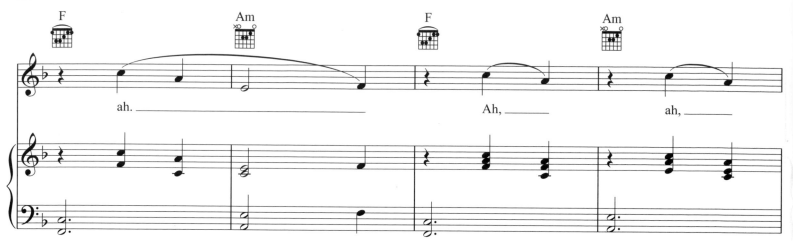

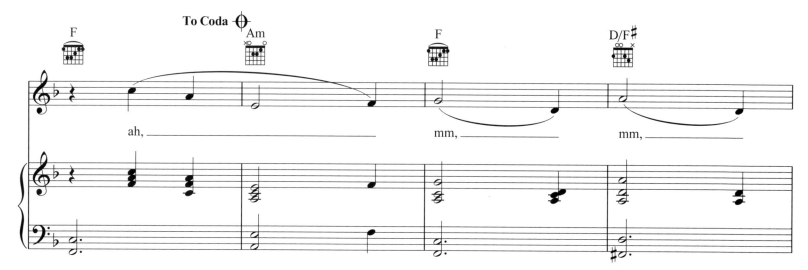

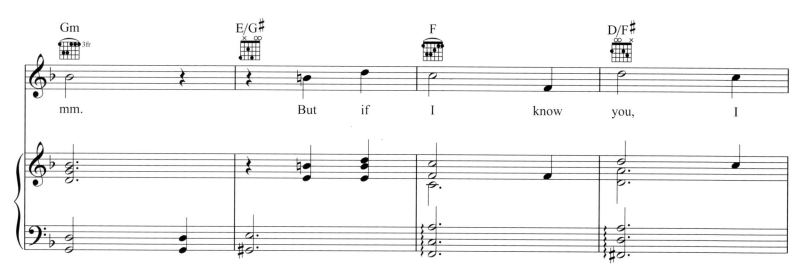

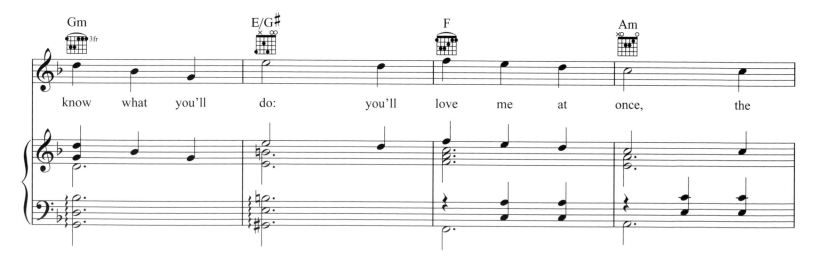

way you did once up - on a

dream.

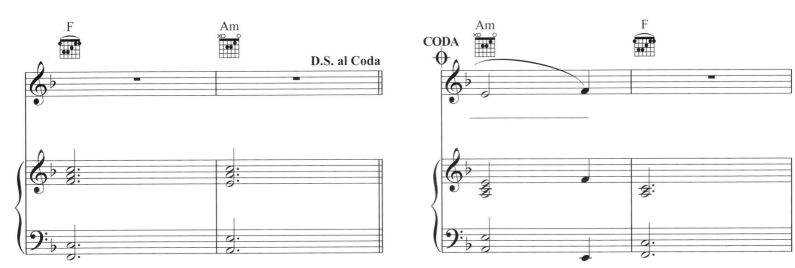

D.S. al Coda

CODA

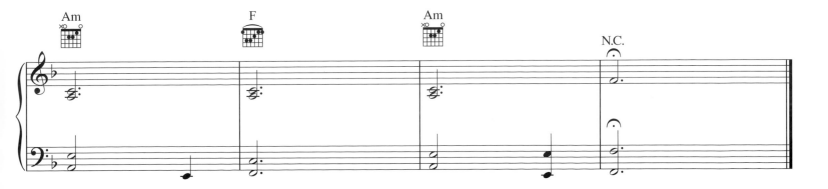

N.C.